NATIONAL
GEOGRAPHIC
KiDS

BRAiN
CANDY

Seriously Sweet Facts
to Satisfy Your Curiosity

NATIONAL GEOGRAPHIC
WASHINGTON, D.C.

HAVE YOU EVER WONDERED ...

Fact-alicious!

... **WHICH IS HOTTER:** the surface of the sun or the core of the Earth?

... **HOW MANY ATOMS YOU'D HAVE TO STACK** to be as wide as one human hair?

... **WHAT COULD HAPPEN IN A BILLION SECONDS,** in a billion hours, or with a billion ... goldfish?

WELCOME TO *BRAIN CANDY*, A SWEET SELECTION OF JUICY TIDBITS, TELLING TRUTHS, UNCANNY CONNECTIONS, AND MIND–BLOWING FACTS.

Each spread in *Brain Candy* will give you a bit of information and then expand on it with related revelations. Light travels at 186,000 miles per second (300,000 km/s). At that speed, you could circle the Earth 7.5 times and get to the galaxy next door in 25,000 years! The tallest volcano in our solar system is on Mars. But just how tall is it? Three times taller than Mount Everest ... and big enough to fit the entire chain of Hawaiian Islands inside! And guess what: There are 10 quintillion insects on the planet. That's sounds like a lot, but it's hard to picture 10 quintillion of anything ... until you learn that it equals more than 200 million insects for every human on the planet!

LIKE LEARNING COOL FACTS AND HOW THEY'RE CONNECTED? *BRAIN CANDY* IS GOING TO BE A TREAT.

A **MILLION** IS A **LOT.**

A **MILLION** ANTS WEIGH AS MUCH AS **ONE HUMAN.**

A **MILLION** **DAYS** AGO THE **FIRST OLYMPICS** WERE TAKING PLACE IN **ANCIENT GREECE.**

IF YOU LIVE A **MILLION** **HOURS,** YOU WILL BE **114** **YEARS OLD.**

A **BILLION SECONDS** IS **11,574 DAYS.**

IT WOULD TAKE A **FOOTBALL-STADIUM-SIZE BOWL** TO HOLD A **BILLION GOLDFISH.**

A **BILLION HOURS AGO,** HUMAN ANCESTORS WERE LIVING IN THE **STONE AGE.**

EVERYONE'S
TASTE BUDS
ARE DIFFERENT.

People have between **2,000** and **10,000** **taste buds.**

Some people have a **gene** that makes **cilantro** taste like **soap.**

Ageusia is the **inability to taste** anything.

Picky eaters— sometimes called **supertasters**— can have up to **twice as many** taste buds as everyone else.

11

BIRTHDAYS
are happening all the time.

MORE THAN **17 MILLION PEOPLE** AROUND THE WORLD CELEBRATE A BIRTHDAY ON ANY GIVEN DAY.

Happy PURR-thday!

BIRTHDAYS HAPPEN SO OFTEN THAT "HAPPY BIRTHDAY TO YOU" IS THE **MOST RECOGNIZED SONG** IN THE ENGLISH LANGUAGE.

IN A GROUP OF 23 PEOPLE, THERE'S A **50–50 CHANCE** THAT TWO OF THEM WILL SHARE THE **SAME BIRTHDAY.**

NINE OF THE TOP 10 MOST **COMMON BIRTHDAYS** IN THE UNITED STATES ARE BETWEEN **SEPTEMBER 9 AND 20.**

YOUR PET CAN GO THE DISTANCE.

That's a SWEET ride!

14

A **LOST DOG** once **walked 2,000 miles** (3,219 km) across Australia to find its way home.

I ♥ AUSTRALIA

A **HAMSTER** can **run up to five miles** (8 km) a night on the wheel in its cage.

DOMESTIC CATS can **wander as far as 1.9 miles** (3 km) from home, one study found.

15

I was born to go FAST...

On straightaways, **NASCAR drivers** can travel **almost the length** of an **American football field** in **one second.**

NASCAR drivers experience about
3 g's of force
on every turn—the same as astronauts during a **space shuttle launch.**

NASCAR IS ALL ABOUT SPEED.

Pit stop crews can change four tires in **12 seconds.**

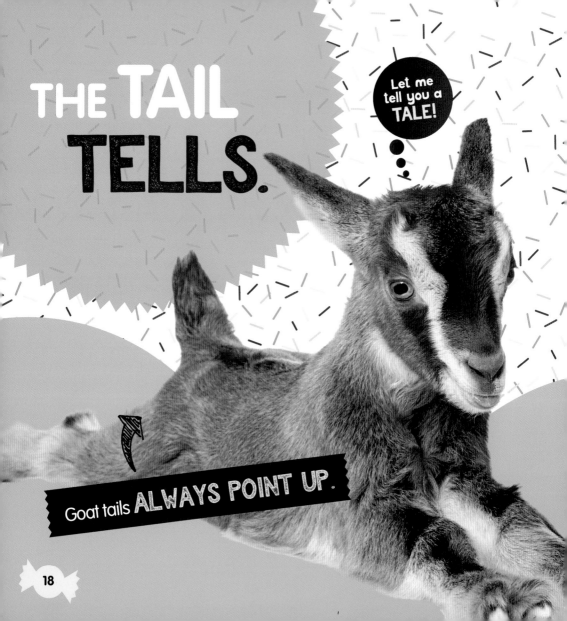

Sheep tails ALWAYS POINT DOWN.

NUMBERS CAN BE BIG—
REALLY BIG.

A **GOOGOL** IS A **1** FOLLOWED BY **100 ZEROS.**

A **GOOGOLPLEX** IS A **1** FOLLOWED BY A **GOOGOL ZEROS.**

That's 10,000,000,000,000,000,000,000,000,000,000,000,000,000, 000,000,000,000,000,000,000,000,000,000,000,000,000,000,000, 000,000,000,000,000.

WRITING A **GOOGOLPLEX** DOWN WOULD **TAKE LONGER** THAN THE AGE OF THE UNIVERSE.

THE LARGEST KNOWN NUMBER, GRAHAM'S NUMBER, IS **SO BIG** THAT WRITING IT DOWN WOULD BE **IMPOSSIBLE.**

21

THERE'S MORE THAN ONE WAY TO EAT PIZZA.

NEW YORK STYLE:
EATEN WITH YOUR HANDS

CHICAGO DEEP-DISH:
EATEN WITH A KNIFE AND A FORK

THE BLUE WHALE IS THE **LARGEST ANIMAL** EVER TO HAVE LIVED ON EARTH.

A BABY COULD **CRAWL** THROUGH A BLUE WHALE'S **BLOWHOLE.**

A TODDLER COULD **SWIM** THROUGH A BLUE WHALE'S **LARGEST VEINS.**

100 PEOPLE COULD FIT IN A BLUE **WHALE'S MOUTH.**

AFRICA IS MUCH BIGGER THAN YOU THINK.

WOW!

Africa is **LARGER THAN** China, India, Eastern Europe, and the U.S.A. combined.

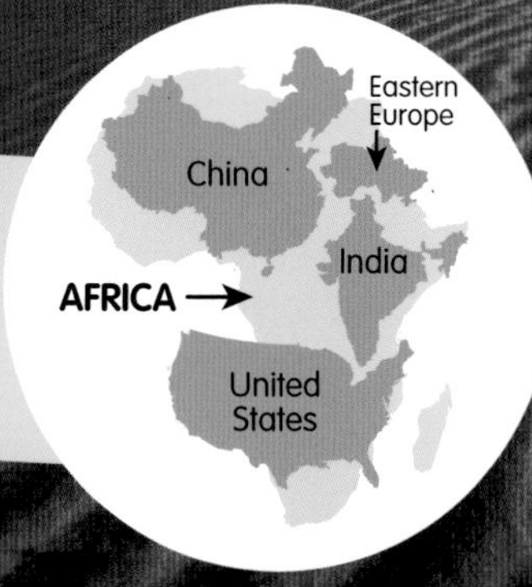

Eastern Europe

China

India

AFRICA →

United States

Africa's Sahara—**THE LARGEST DESERT IN THE WORLD**—is bigger than the entire continental United States.

Although Africa is **14 TIMES LARGER** than Greenland, they often appear the same size on maps.

AFRICA

Greenland

Africa is **ALMOST TWICE THE SIZE** of Russia.

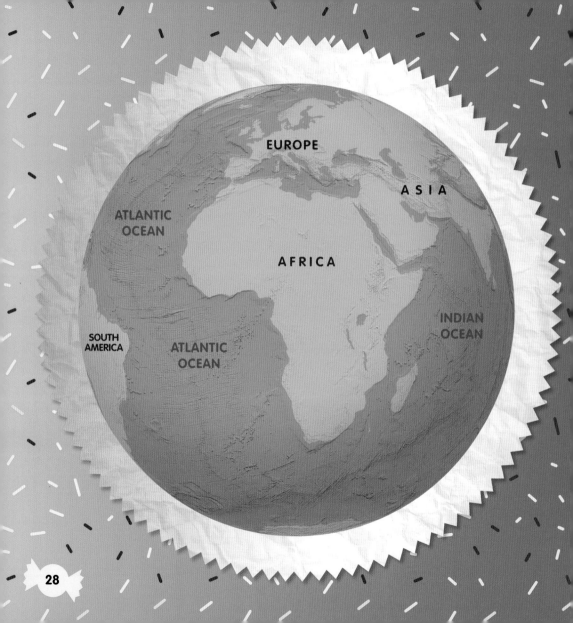

EUROPE

ASIA

ATLANTIC
OCEAN

AFRICA

INDIAN
OCEAN

SOUTH
AMERICA

ATLANTIC
OCEAN

WHY DO MAPS LIE?

Maps aren't something we question as being right or wrong. We believe that what we are looking at on paper is exactly as it would appear if we flew over it in an airplane. But maps lie—because they have to. Here's why: Earth is a sphere. A globe gives us the most accurate representation of what the world looks like, but sometimes we need to look at it flattened out—on paper. So mapmakers have a trick to solve that problem: They translate a sphere using something called projection. The most common is the Mercator projection. Created in the 16th century, it worked perfectly for measuring nautical distances, but it stretched the northern and southern poles upward, making Africa and South America appear smaller than they actually are. And here's another way maps lie: Since the first Mercator projection, maps have been generally made with north facing up—the North Pole is at the top of a world map, and Antarctica is at the bottom. But there's no scientific reason for north to be the "roof of the world." In ancient Egyptian times, the top of the world was portrayed as being in the east. Early Islamic maps positioned south at the top. What's up and what's down is really all a matter of perspective!

... Pants on FIRE!

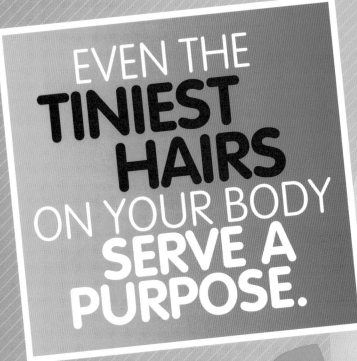

EVEN THE TINIEST HAIRS ON YOUR BODY SERVE A PURPOSE.

Your **EYELASHES** **protect your eyes** from the wind.

Your **EYEBROW HAIRS** **shield your eyes** from sweat.

I'm EXTRA protected!

Your **NOSE HAIRS** defend against dirt, pollen, and germs.

31

PEOPLE GO NUTTY FOR NOODLES.

More than **100 BILLION SERVINGS** of **instant noodles** are eaten every year worldwide.

A theater in Japan is shaped like an **INSTANT NOODLES CUP.**

Oh, the longest NOODLE!

The **LONGEST NOODLE EVER MADE** was about **2 miles (3.2 km) long.**

THE **OCEAN** IS **REALLY DEEP.**

HELLO?
Anybody
home?

MOUNT EVEREST COULD **SIT AT THE DEEPEST POINT** IN THE OCEAN AND STILL BE **MORE THAN A MILE** (1.6 KM) **BELOW** THE SURFACE.

THE **DEEPEST PART** OF THE OCEAN— **CHALLENGER DEEP**—IS **FARTHER AWAY FROM THE SURFACE** THAN AN AIRPLANE AT **CRUISING ALTITUDE.**

THE **PRESSURE** AT THE **OCEAN'S DEEPEST POINT** WOULD BE COMPARABLE TO BALANCING A **2,200-POUND (1,000-KG) WEIGHT** ON **THE TIP OF YOUR FINGER.**

FOUR TIMES AS MANY PEOPLE HAVE **WALKED ON THE MOON** AS HAVE BEEN TO THE **BOTTOM OF THE OCEAN.**

This gives new meaning to "HOT DOG!"

IT'S GETTING HOT OUT HERE.

The temperature at the **surface of the sun** is

10,000°F (5500°C).

Earth's core is believed to be **just as hot.**

But the **air around a lightning bolt** is **five times hotter.**

And a **supernova** is even hotter—**10,000 times hotter** than the sun.

37

ALCATRAZ IS AN INFAMOUS ISLAND.

California, U.S.A.'s **ALCATRAZ ISLAND** was once a prison for America's most **NOTORIOUS CRIMINALS.**

In the 1930s, Alcatraz housed infamous mobster **AL CAPONE,** who played **BANJO** in the inmate band.

NO PRISONERS were ever confirmed to have escaped from Alcatraz.

Alcatraz is rumored to be one of the **MOST HAUNTED PLACES** in the United States.

PEOPLE TAKE A LOT OF PHOTOS.

EVERY DAY,
93 MILLION
SELFIES ARE
SNAPPED.

THAT'S
**33 BILLION,
945 MILLION**
SELFIES
A **YEAR.**

MORE THAN
**ONE TRILLION
PHOTOS**
ARE TAKEN
ANNUALLY.

TIME IS RELATIVE.

A DAY ON JUPITER IS
10 EARTH HOURS.

A YEAR ON JUPITER IS
12 EARTH YEARS.

42

I finally had my **FIRST** birthday!

43

Inventors find **INSPIRATION** in unexpected places.

SCIENTISTS MADE **LED LIGHTS** 55 PERCENT BRIGHTER AFTER THEY MIMICKED THE JAGGED SCALES ON A **FIREFLY'S LANTERN.**

THE DRAG-REDUCING **WARTY RIDGES** ON THE EDGE OF HUMPBACK WHALES' FINS INSPIRED MORE EFFICIENT **WIND TURBINES.**

A **JAPANESE BULLET TRAIN'S** STREAMLINED NOSE WAS MODELED AFTER A **KINGFISHER'S BEAK** TO MAKE IT QUIETER IN TUNNELS.

SCIENTISTS STUDIED HOW **NAMIBIAN BEETLES** COLLECT DEW ON THEIR BACKS TO MAKE **WATER COLLECTING SYSTEMS** IN DESERTS.

Where's the TUNA?

Your grocery store is all mixed up.

Strawberries, raspberries, and blackberries **AREN'T REALLY BERRIES.**

But bananas, eggplants, chili peppers, and oranges ARE BERRIES.

Tomatoes, bell peppers, avocados, green peas, and okra are all technically FRUITS, not vegetables.

Peanuts, almonds, pecans, and cashews aren't actually nuts; they're SEEDS.

THERE ARE MORE THAN

SEVEN BILLION

PEOPLE LIVING ON EARTH.

IF **EVERYONE ON THE PLANET** STOOD **SHOULDER TO SHOULDER,** WE WOULD FIT IN THE CITY OF **LOS ANGELES.**

IF **ALL THE WORLD'S PEOPLE** WERE **STACKED HEAD TO TOE**, WE WOULD REACH ABOUT **1/14** OF THE WAY TO **THE SUN.**

IF EVERYONE **LIVED AS CLOSE TOGETHER** AS PEOPLE DO IN **NEW YORK CITY,** THE WORLD'S POPULATION COULD FIT IN **NEW ZEALAND.**

IF EVERYONE **LIVED AS FAR APART** AS PEOPLE DO IN **ALASKA, U.S.A.,** WE'D NEED **108 PLANETS** TO FIT EVERYONE.

DOGS HAVE SUPER SENSES ...

They **smell** separately with **each nostril,** helping them figure out where **smells are coming from.**

They have **special taste buds** specifically devoted to **water.**

They can **hear sounds four times farther away** than humans can.

Their **entire bodies** are covered with **touch-sensitive nerve endings.**

Belly rubs, PLEASE!

51

You can
PET ME
now ...

... AND CATS HAVE SUPER SENSES, TOO.

They can **ROTATE THEIR EARS** **180** DEGREES.

They have **WHISKERS ON THEIR ELBOWS** that pick up vibrations and breezes.

They **SWEAT** from their **PAW PADS.**

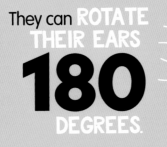

They can see up to **EIGHT TIMES BETTER IN THE DARK** than humans can.

Roller coasters are THRILLING.

A PERSON'S **HEART RACES FASTEST** RIGHT BEFORE—NOT DURING—A **BIG DROP** ON A ROLLER COASTER.

RIDERS ON SOUTH AFRICA'S TOWER OF TERROR EXPERIENCE **TWICE THE G-FORCE** THAT ASTRONAUTS DID DURING THE **LAUNCH OF THE SPACE SHUTTLE.**

THE **FASTEST ROLLER COASTER** IN THE WORLD GOES **TWICE AS FAST** AS A CAR BARRELING DOWN A HIGHWAY.

55

ANIMALS CAN BE SMALL BUT

DEADLY.

THE **FANGS** OF THE **SYDNEY FUNNEL-WEB SPIDER** ARE CAPABLE OF **PIERCING THROUGH FINGERNAILS.**

CONE SNAILS DELIVER **TOXIC VENOM** THROUGH A HARPOON-LIKE **TOOTH.**

BITES FROM AFRICA'S **BLOODSUCKING TSETSE FLY** CAUSE A POTENTIALLY DEADLY **SLEEPING SICKNESS.**

THE **BLUE-RINGED OCTOPUS** IS THE SIZE OF A GOLF BALL BUT PACKS ENOUGH **VENOM** TO KILL **26 PEOPLE.**

THE **HARE** REALLY SHOULD HAVE BEATEN THE **TORTOISE.**

58

HARES ARE SO SPEEDY THEY COULD OUTRUN USAIN BOLT, THE WORLD'S FASTEST HUMAN.

TORTOISES ARE SO SLOW IT WOULD TAKE THEM MORE THAN FOUR HOURS TO GO A SINGLE MILE (1.6 KM).

SLOW poke!

59

WORLD LEADERS HAVE HAD REGULAR JOBS.

QUEEN ELIZABETH II was a **TRUCK MECHANIC** during **WORLD WAR II.**

A **FORMER DJ** became **PRESIDENT OF MADAGASCAR.**

U.S. president **BARACK OBAMA'S FIRST JOB** was scooping **ICE CREAM.**

POPE FRANCIS once worked **SECURITY** at a nightclub.

AUSTRALIA IS FAMOUS
FOR ITS BEACHES ....

You could visit **A NEW ONE** every day for more than **29 YEARS**.

But before **1902** it was **ILLEGAL TO SWIM** in Australia's surf during daytime hours.

Even still, **70 PERCENT** of the country is **DESERT.**

Australia's **HYAMS BEACH** holds the world record for the **WHITEST BEACH SAND** on **EARTH.**

It would take you **37 WEEKS** to **WALK THE COASTLINE** of the Australian continent's mainland.

UNUSUAL ANIMALS.

KANGAROOS can **SWIM** but they can't **JUMP** BACKWARD.

The **DUCK-BILLED PLATYPUS** is one of only two mammal species that **LAY EGGS** to reproduce.

TERMITE-EATING TURTLE FROGS— one of the few frog species that **SKIP** the **TADPOLE STAGE**—look like shell-less turtles.

Inland taipan

Hi.
FRIENDSSS!

ISLAND OF DANGEROUS ANIMALS

Australia is home to lots of deadly species. This island nation—the only country that is also a continent—takes the prize for the world's most venomous snakes. Drop for drop, the eight-foot (2.5-m)-long inland taipan, also known as the fierce snake, produces the most toxic venom of any snake in the world. It may be the most venomous snake on the planet, but it's not really the most dangerous: This reclusive reptile typically keeps to itself in its remote home in southwestern Queensland and northeastern South Australia. Australia also harbors deadly spiders and sea creatures. But what's the most bizarre poisonous creature of all found only in Australia? The duck-billed platypus. Yes, this egg-laying mammal, with a bill and feet like a duck, a tail like a beaver, and fur like an otter, is actually venomous! Males of the species have spurs on their rear feet that they use to inflict a toxic blow when defending themselves against enemies or asserting themselves when competing with one another for mates. Although it would be pretty painful to be on the other end of a platypus spur, its venom is not considered dangerous to humans.

Platypus spur

Duck-billed platypus

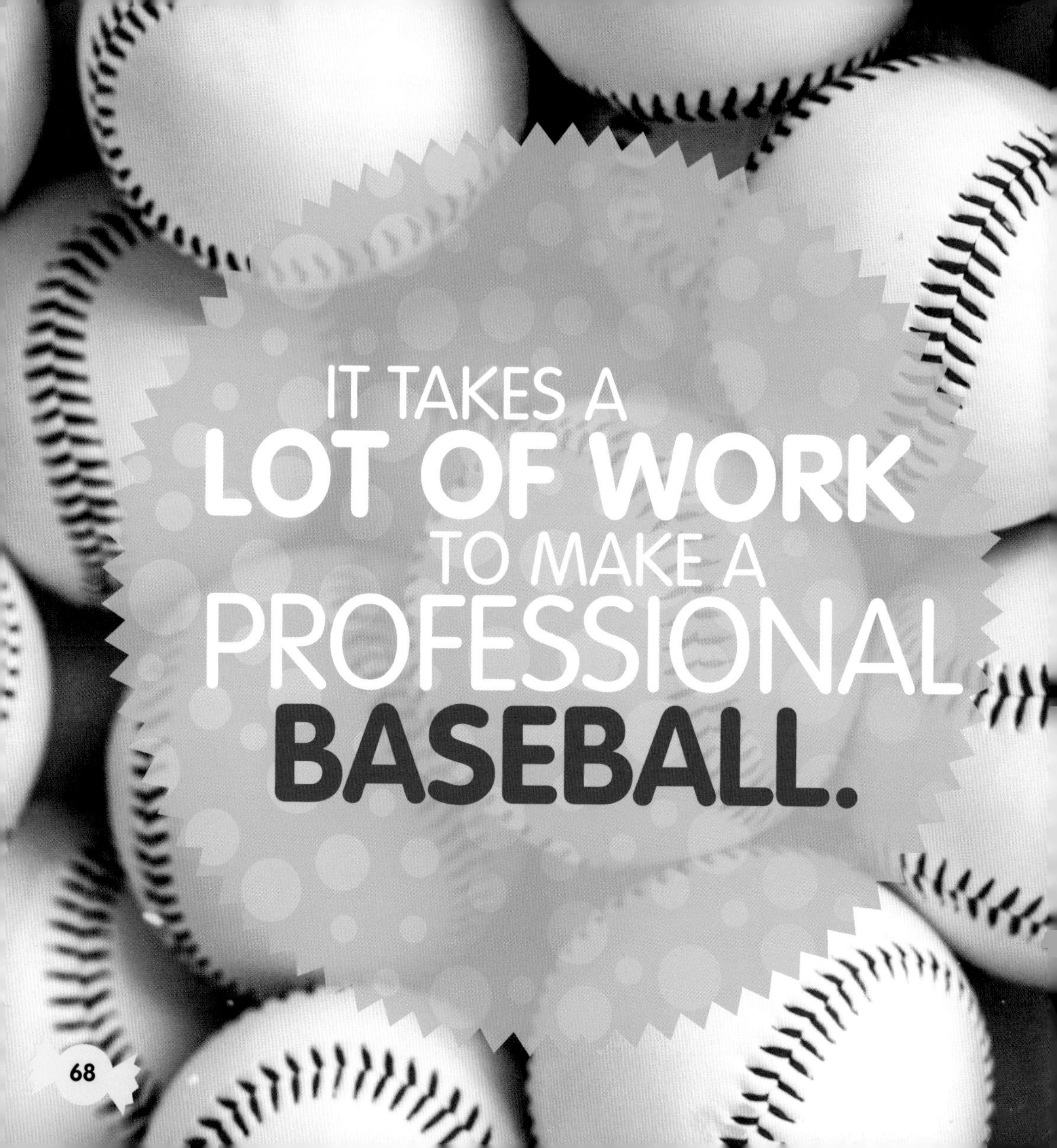

IT TAKES A
LOT OF WORK
TO MAKE A
PROFESSIONAL
BASEBALL.

There are **108 stitches** on a **major league baseball.**

Each ball is **stitched by hand.**

Every major league baseball is **rubbed with special mud** from the Delaware River before it's used.

THE FIRST COMIC BOOK FEATURING SUPERMAN SOLD FOR

10 CENTS

WHEN IT WAS PUBLISHED IN 1938.

A COPY OF THAT COMIC SOLD FOR

$3.2 MILLION

AT AN AUCTION IN 2014—THE HIGHEST PRICE EVER PAID FOR A COMIC.

SOME ANIMALS

GLOW

IN THE DARK.

Anglerfish

VAMPIRE SQUID EJECT **BIOLUMINESCENT MUCUS** FROM THEIR ARMS TO **DEFEND THEMSELVES.**

FIREFLIES GLOW TO HELP THEM FIND A **MATE.**

You make me GLOW with joy!

MORE THAN **80 PERCENT** OF DEEP-SEA CREATURES ARE **BIOLUMINESCENT.**

Cycloseris erosa coral

SOME MILLIPEDES GLOW UNDER **BLACK LIGHT.**

Mandarin fish

RUBBER DUCKS DO MORE THAN JUST FLOAT IN THE TUB.

A five-story inflated yellow duck **TRAVELS TO CITY HARBORS** around the world.

They **STARRED ON TELEVISION** when Ernie from *Sesame Street* made the song "Rubber Duckie" a hit.

In 1992, a crate with 28,000 rubber ducks **FELL OFF A CARGO SHIP** in the North Pacific.

Scientists have been tracking them to learn about **OCEAN CURRENTS.**

FOOD
IS FOR MORE THAN JUST EATING.

I'm feeling TOASTY!

Rye bread can
WIPE SMUDGES OFF WALLS.

Cold plain yogurt can relieve
SUNBURN PAIN.

Banana peels can
SHINE SILVER.

ANIMALS CAN HAVE UNEXPECTED RELATIVES.

HYENAS ARE MORE CLOSELY RELATED TO CATS THAN TO DOGS.

ELEPHANTS' CLOSEST LIVING RELATIVES ARE MANATEES.

Time for a family REUNION!

A LOT CAN HAPPEN IN

ONE MINUTE.

IN SIXTY SECONDS ...

... A **HUMMINGBIRD** CAN **FLAP ITS WINGS** AROUND **4,000 TIMES.**

... **189,600 TONS** (172,000 T) OF **WATER** FLOW OVER **NIAGARA FALLS.**

... YOU WILL **BLINK 15 TO 20 TIMES.**

... THE **CURRENT WORLD CHAMPION** CAN **SOLVE A RUBIK'S CUBE 12 TIMES.**

... THE **AVERAGE THIRD GRADER** CAN **READ** ABOUT **150 WORDS.**

Taking care
of your
TEETH
used to be
a pain.

82

PUCKER UP!

DURING THE MIDDLE AGES, PEOPLE THOUGHT **KISSING A DONKEY** HELPED RELIEVE A **TOOTHACHE**.

DIVERS EXPLORING A 17TH-CENTURY SHIPWRECK FOUND A **GOLDEN TOOL** THAT WAS BOTH A **TOOTHPICK** AND AN **EARWAX SPOON**.

ANCIENT EGYPTIANS USED TOOTHPASTE MADE OF **OX HOOVES** AND **BURNT EGGSHELLS**.

BRISTLES ON THE FIRST TOOTHBRUSHES WERE MADE FROM **PIG HAIR**.

SOUND TRAVELS
REALLY QUICKLY.

The speed of sound is about **767 MILES AN HOUR** (1,235 km/h).

Sound travels
**FOUR TIMES
FASTER**
through water
than through air ...

... and
**TEN TIMES
FASTER**
through wood
than through air.

85

AIRPLANES HAVE COME A LONG WAY ...

The **first flight** lasted just **12 SECONDS.**

That's $\frac{1}{1,470}$ as long as a flight from **Los Angeles to New York City.**

LES → NEW YORK
6, 2017

LAX
12:00 PM

JFK
4:15 PM

BOARDING
11:45 AM

FLIGHT
BC463

GATE
8A

SEAT
17B

Again, **AGAIN!**

Today the **world's biggest passenger plane,** the Airbus A380, can carry up to **853 PEOPLE.**

The **first flying airplane** could hold only **one** of its two inventors.

... AND SO HAVE

COMPUTERS.

My name is WOODY!

THE **FIRST COMPUTER MOUSE** WAS **MADE OF WOOD.**

THE **FIRST PROGRAMMABLE DIGITAL COMPUTER** WEIGHED 30 TONS (27 T) AND **TOOK UP AN ENTIRE ROOM.**

TODAY'S TINIEST **COMPUTER** IS THE SIZE OF A **GRAIN OF RICE.**

THE REAL-LIFE
BATMAN

Click! Clicky click! Clickety-click-click-click! What's that?
You don't speak bat? You could! Scientists have found that humans can actually learn echolocation, which is the way bats and dolphins (and some other animals) make sounds and use the echoes of those sounds to navigate the world around them.

Bats use echolocation to "see" prey as they hunt at night. Humans who were born without the ability to see or who have lost their vision can use sound in the same way. A man named Daniel Kish, who lost his sight as a baby, uses fast tongue clicks—two or three per second—to get around. His nickname is the "real-life Batman," because he uses the same technique that bats use to navigate in the dark. He can uncover important details about a place using these clicks, like whether objects in a room are big or small, and made of metal or wood. Because he can "see" so well, he is able to do things—such as hiking—that would otherwise be difficult. Even people with perfect vision can learn this skill.

Daniel Kish

THE **LARGEST MOUNTAIN** ON EARTH IS A **VOLCANO** THAT'S MOSTLY **UNDERWATER.**

Hawaii's **Mauna Loa** is **56,330 FEET** (17,170 m) from **base to top,** but three-quarters of it is below the **ocean's surface.**

Mount Everest

From its peak to its base, **Mauna Loa** is

ALMOST TWICE AS TALL as **MOUNT EVEREST,** the tallest mountain on Earth above sea level.

Mauna Loa is so heavy that the **ocean floor beneath it has sunk 26,000 FEET** (8,000 m).

THE TALLEST
KNOWN MOUNTAIN IN OUR
SOLAR SYSTEM IS A

VOLCANO
ON MARS.

Olympus Mons is 16 miles (26 km) high—about **three times taller** than **Mount Everest.**

Hello my name is

Olympus Mons

Olympus Mons is about as **wide** as the **U.S. state** of **Arizona.**

The **entire chain** of **Hawaiian Islands** could **fit inside** Olympus Mons.

THERE ARE **10 QUINTILLION** (10,000,000,000,000,000,000) INDIVIDUAL **INSECTS ALIVE ON EARTH.**

Insects make up **80 PERCENT** of the world's species.

There are more than **200 MILLION INSECTS** for every human on the planet.

A total of **26 MILLION** insects live in every square mile (2.6 sq km) of habitable land on Earth.

Locust swarms can contain as many as **ONE BILLION** individuals.

East African termite queens can lay an egg every **TWO SECONDS.**

That's 43,200 eggs in one day!

97

THE STATE OF ALASKA IS

REALLY BIG...

ALASKA IS **BIGGER** THAN CALIFORNIA, TEXAS, AND MONTANA **COMBINED.**

MORE THAN HALF OF THE ENTIRE **U.S. COASTLINE** IS IN **ALASKA.**

IT WOULD TAKE JUST OVER **FIVE ALASKAS** TO FIT INTO THE CONTINENTAL **UNITED STATES.**

IF ALASKA WERE A **COUNTRY,** IT WOULD BE THE **33rd LARGEST** IN THE WORLD.

HELLO? Anybody home?

99

... AND THE STATE OF **RHODE ISLAND** IS REALLY SMALL.

COZY!

Rhode Island is **so small** it could **fit into Alaska** **425 times.**

The **second smallest state** (Delaware) is still **nearly twice** Rhode Island's size.

It takes only **about an hour** to **drive across the whole state.**

Greetings from

RHODE ISLAND

USA

102

UNICORNS **ARE** REAL (SORT OF).

The **NARWHAL** is often called "**THE UNICORN OF THE SEA**" thanks to its long, pointy tooth (tusk).

People used to buy powdered "**UNICORN HORN**," believing it was an antidote to poison. (It was actually the **TOOTH OF THE NARWHAL**.)

The unicorn is the **NATIONAL ANIMAL** of Scotland.

Shaggy "**SIBERIAN UNICORNS**"— actually members of an extinct species of rhinoceros—roamed Asia 29,000 years ago.

Birds
are
AMAZING
animals.

FLAMINGOS CAN ONLY EAT **UPSIDE DOWN.**

COMMON SWIFTS CAN SPEND UP TO **10 MONTHS** IN FLIGHT.

CHICKENS ARE THE CLOSEST LIVING RELATIVES OF **T. REX.**

A FRIGATEBIRD CAN SOAR FOR **40 MILES** (64 km) WITHOUT FLAPPING ITS WINGS.

AN AFRICAN GRAY PARROT IS ABOUT AS SMART AS A **THREE-YEAR-OLD KID.**

EATING
IN SPACE
ISN'T EASY.

BREAD IS BANNED ON THE INTERNATIONAL SPACE STATION BECAUSE **FLOATING CRUMBS** COULD GET IN **ASTRONAUTS' EYES.**

SOME ASTRONAUTS ADD **HOT SAUCE** TO THEIR FOOD BECAUSE **MICROGRAVITY** DULLS THEIR **SENSE OF TASTE.**

ASTRONAUTS DRINK A FILTERED MIX OF **RECYCLED SHOWER WATER, URINE, AND SWEAT.**

IN 1965, AN **AMERICAN ASTRONAUT SMUGGLED** A **CORNED-BEEF SANDWICH** ABOARD A **SPACEFLIGHT.**

No SLEEP-WALKING here!

HACKS

When astronauts leave Earth for the International Space Station, they leave gravity behind too. Microgravity—where gravity is very weak—makes everyday activities in the International Space Station a challenge. Imagine going to the bathroom and immediately floating right off the toilet! *Awkward.* Astronauts must put on a seat belt to stay put until they're, ahem, done. Even sleeping brings challenges. Instead of covering up with blankets, which would float away, astronauts have to crawl into sleeping bags that are attached to a wall. Even something as simple as making a sandwich is a challenge in space: Crumbs can lead to big problems on the International Space Station if they float away and get stuck in equipment. The solution? Astronauts substitute tortillas for bread. And sandwich staples like peanut butter and jelly are squeezed out of tubes to make spreading easy. Setting the table for a meal in a place where everything floats isn't typical either. Tools like scissors to open squeeze tubes are connected to a tether and attached to a wall or table, while other objects like cups and utensils stay put with the help of Velcro. Problem-solving is an important job requirement for astronauts.

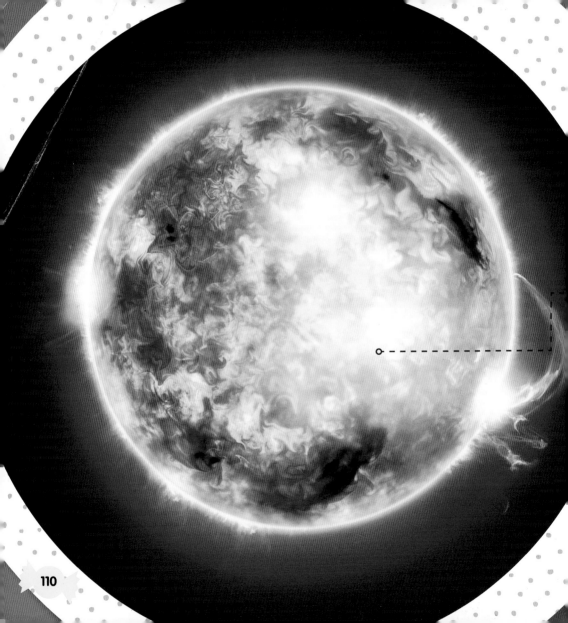

THE SUN IS THE CLOSEST STAR TO EARTH.

Going **60 MILES** an hour (96.5 km/h), it would take about **177 YEARS TO DRIVE TO THE SUN.**

EVERY STAR in the night sky is **BRIGHTER** than the **SUN,** but the sun appears to be the **BRIGHTEST** because it's so close.

The next closest stars to Earth are **ALPHA CENTAURI A AND B.** It takes about **4.3 YEARS** for **LIGHT** from these stars to reach Earth; it takes only **8 MINUTES** and **20 SECONDS** from the sun.

SHOES AND HUMANS ARE "SOLE" MATES.

People have been wearing shoes for **40,000 YEARS.**

The world's oldest leather shoe is **1,000 YEARS OLDER** than the Great Pyramids of Giza.

Shoes **CHANGED THE WAY** humans walk.

Until the 1800s, there was **NO DIFFERENCE** between a right shoe and a left shoe.

113

MORE THAN **50 PERCENT** OF AMERICANS **KNOCK ON WOOD** TO **AVOID BAD LUCK.**

IN SPAIN, PEOPLE **EAT 12 GRAPES** AT MIDNIGHT ON **NEW YEAR'S EVE** TO HAVE **GOOD LUCK** THROUGHOUT THE YEAR.

IN SOME COUNTRIES IT'S **BAD LUCK** TO **TRIM YOUR FINGERNAILS** OR TOENAILS **AFTER DARK.**

IN SOME CULTURES, **FISH** ARE SYMBOLS OF **GOOD LUCK** AND **WEALTH.**

That's a lot of MOUTHS to feed!

NATURE'S **NURSERY** IS A **WILD PLACE.**

Some octopuses lay up to **100,000 EGGS** at a time.

Koala babies eat their mothers' poop until they're old enough to DIGEST FOOD on their own.

When they're born, baby elephants **WEIGH ABOUT 200 POUNDS** (91 kg).

YOUR BODY DOES **IMPORTANT THINGS**– EVEN WHEN YOU'RE NOT PAYING ATTENTION. **EVERY DAY ...**

... your **heart beats** about

100,000 times.

... you **shed** about **35,000 dead skin cells.**

... you **take** about

23,000 breaths.

... you **make 34 to 68 ounces** (1 to 2 L) **of spit.**

119

Ants are PICKY.

ANTS THAT LIVE **MORE THAN 60 MILES** (100 KM) FROM THE **OCEAN PREFER SALTY** OVER SWEET FOODS.

I only eat ORGANIC.

ANTS DON'T LIKE THE **SMELL** OF **LEMON.**

SOME ANTS PREFER THE **SMELL** OF **HONEYDEW** OVER OTHER SWEET THINGS.

HUMANS ARE **STILL** EVOLVING.

WE'RE TALLER NOW than we were 150 years ago.

DUTCH PEOPLE HAVE GROWN THE MOST— about seven inches (18 cm) on average.

OUR HEADS HAVE GOTTEN BIGGER to hold bigger brains.

Some people are now **BORN WITHOUT VESTIGIAL BODY PARTS** (things that no longer serve a purpose) like an appendix or wisdom teeth.

PREHISTORIC ANIMALS WERE

HUGE.

MEGATHERIUM AMERICANUM, A GIANT AVOCADO-EATING **GROUND SLOTH** FROM **SOUTH AMERICA,** WEIGHED MORE THAN **FOUR TONS** (3.6 T) AND WAS **AS LONG AS AN SUV.**

TITANOBOA, THE **LARGEST SNAKE EVER,** WAS AS **LONG AS A SCHOOL BUS** AND AS **WIDE AS A TRUCK TIRE.**

THE **WORLD'S LARGEST RODENT EVER—** APPROPRIATELY CALLED **MEGARODENT—**WAS **LARGER THAN A BISON** AND **FOUGHT OFF SABER-TOOTHED CATS** IN SOUTH AMERICA'S RAINFORESTS.

125

SKYSCRAPERS COME
in many sizes.

It would take more than **15** of the **WORLD'S SMALLEST SKYSCRAPER,** in Wichita Falls, Texas, U.S.A., to reach the top of the **Space Needle** in Seattle, Washington, U.S.A.

But you'd have to stack nearly **TWO** Empire State Buildings to measure up to the **Burj Khalifa** in Dubai, U.A.E., the **WORLD'S TALLEST BUILDING.**

The Space Needle is less than **HALF THE HEIGHT** of the **Empire State Building** in New York City.

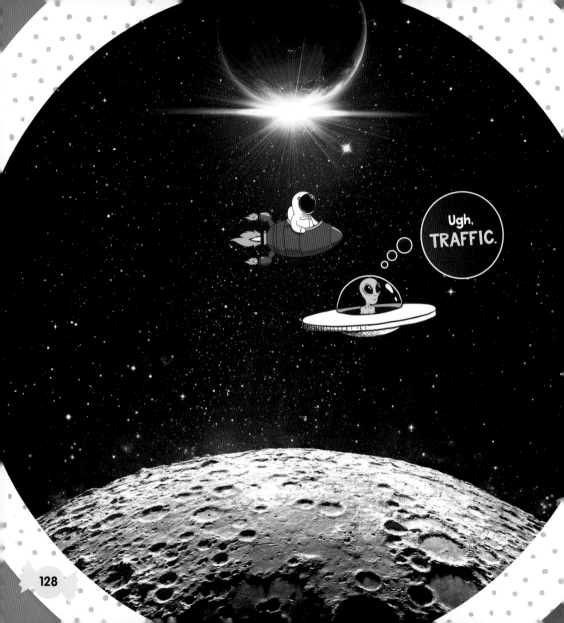

THE MOON IS AN AVERAGE OF

238,855

MILES (384,399 KM) AWAY FROM EARTH.

All our **SOLAR SYSTEM'S PLANETS** could **FIT IN THE DISTANCE** between Earth and the moon.

If you **LINED UP** all of **EARTH'S BEACHES** end to end, they would **REACH THE MOON.**

It took about **THREE DAYS** for the **FIRST ASTRONAUTS** who **WALKED** on the **MOON** to get there.

If you could **WALK TO THE MOON,** it would take you **NINE YEARS.**

129

WORDS
ARE
WACKY.

IT'S BEEN ESTIMATED THAT A **NEW WORD IS CREATED** EVERY **98 MINUTES.**

WEBSTER'S ONCE PUBLISHED A **DICTIONARY** ACCIDENTALLY FEATURING THE **MADE-UP WORD "DORD."**

DICTIONARY
OF THE ENGLISH LANGUAGE

"MONTH," "PURPLE," AND **"WALRUS" DON'T RHYME** WITH ANY OTHER ENGLISH WORDS.

"SWIMS" IS STILL "SWIMS" EVEN WHEN YOU TURN IT **UPSIDE DOWN.**

¡DORD!

Ernest Vincent
Wright

STAY OUT
OF IT

Think about how much time it takes you to finish writing a book report. Now think about how long it would take you if you weren't allowed to use the letter e. A lot longer, probably!

In 1939, author Ernest Vincent Wright self-published a book called *Gadsby* that included 50,000 words—not one of them contained an e. No "he," "she," "the," or any other word or form of a word containing the fifth letter of the alphabet. To complete his story, Wright had to tie down the "e" button on his typewriter so that the vowel couldn't accidentally slip in. Though the book wasn't popular at the time, it's celebrated now as a major accomplishment.

Should have called it *CATSBY*...

A STYLE OF WRITING THAT DELIBERATELY **OMITS A LETTER** OR LETTERS IS CALLED **A LIPOGRAM.**

THERE ARE MORE WAYS TO CATCH A COLD THAN THE FLU.

There are only **three types** of **flu viruses,** but ...

This
BLOWS ...

... more than
200 types of
viruses can cause a
**common
cold.**

FIREWORKS
HAVE BEEN AROUND FOR A
LONG TIME.

The Chinese first created them **2,000 YEARS AGO** by throwing bamboo into a fire.

Henry the VII of England had fireworks at his wedding in **1486.**

HENRY VII
1485–1509

1ST

On America's first Fourth of July celebration, in **1777,** all the fireworks were orange.

PEOPLE **GET A KICK** OUT OF SOCCER.

Kids in a **fishing village** in **Thailand** play soccer on a **floating field.**

A former **Romanian** soccer player wore his **underwear** inside out for **good luck** on game days.

At the annual **Robocup,** hundreds of **six-inch** (15-cm)-tall **robots** from around the world face off in **soccer matches.**

SOME REPTILES CAN

FLY.

WHEN **DRACO LIZARDS LEAP THROUGH THE AIR,** SKIN BETWEEN THEIR RIBS **OPENS LIKE AN UMBRELLA.**

PTEROSAURS FLEW 78 MILLION YEARS BEFORE **BIRDS DID.**

FLYING SNAKES CAN **GLIDE** THE LENGTH OF **A SOCCER FIELD.**

PEOPLE EAT A LOT OF HOT DOGS.

HOTDOGS

Americans eat an estimated
20 BILLION
hot dogs every year.

You're the **WEINER!**

The world record for the most hot dogs eaten is **72** in **10 MINUTES.**

INVENTED IN 1484, hot dogs have been eaten since **before** the United States existed.

ENJOY OUR
Delicious
25¢
Hot Dogs

BEST IN TOWN!

THE ARCTIC IS SO

COLD...

... **ARCTIC FISH** MAKE THEIR OWN **"ANTIFREEZE"** TO KEEP THEIR BLOOD FROM FREEZING.

... THE AVERAGE WINTER **ARCTIC TEMPERATURE** IS **MINUS 40°F** (-40°C).

... A **VAULT BUILT** INTO A FROZEN ARCTIC MOUNTAIN CAN SAFELY STORE THE SEEDS OF MORE THAN **930,000** FOOD CROPS.

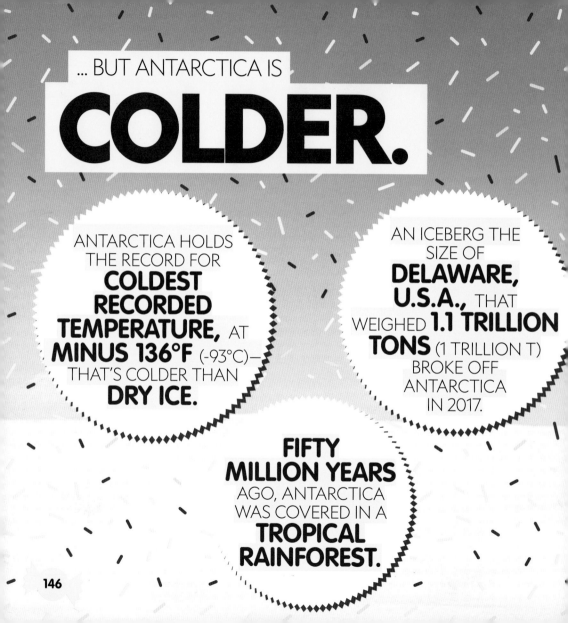

... BUT ANTARCTICA IS

COLDER.

ANTARCTICA HOLDS THE RECORD FOR **COLDEST RECORDED TEMPERATURE,** AT **MINUS 136°F** (-93°C)—THAT'S COLDER THAN **DRY ICE.**

AN ICEBERG THE SIZE OF **DELAWARE, U.S.A.,** THAT WEIGHED **1.1 TRILLION TONS** (1 TRILLION T) BROKE OFF ANTARCTICA IN 2017.

FIFTY MILLION YEARS AGO, ANTARCTICA WAS COVERED IN A **TROPICAL RAINFOREST.**

A TROPICAL VACATION sounds nice...

147

POTATOES AND TOMATOES ARE A DYNAMIC DUO.

Time to KETCHUP to the bad guy!

A British company created a **HYBRID TOMATO PLANT** that grows **tomatoes** on top and **potatoes** on the bottom.

Potatoes and tomatoes are both part of the **NIGHTSHADE FAMILY.**

Americans consume **MORE POTATOES** than any other vegetable. The second most popular vegetable? The tomato (which is technically a fruit).

PEOPLE
PRODUCE **TONS** OF
TRASH.

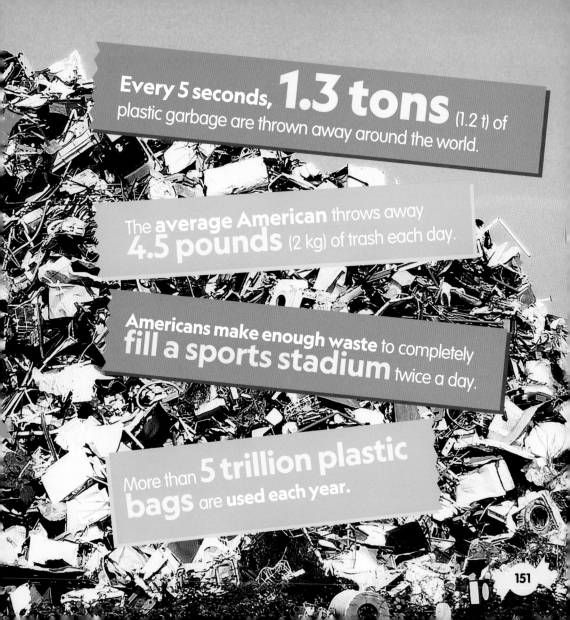

Every 5 seconds, **1.3 tons** (1.2 t) of plastic garbage are thrown away around the world.

The **average American** throws away **4.5 pounds** (2 kg) of trash each day.

Americans make enough waste to completely **fill a sports stadium** twice a day.

More than **5 trillion plastic bags** are **used each year.**

IN YOUR
LIFETIME
YOU WILL ...

... **YAWN** SOME **250,000 TIMES.**

... **EAT** MORE THAN 2,000 POUNDS (907 KG) OF **PIZZA.**

... **READ** MORE THAN **1,000 BOOKS.**

... **BRUSH YOUR TEETH** FOR ABOUT **43 DAYS.**

CLOUDS ARE WILD.

A TYPICAL CUMULUS CLOUD **WEIGHS** AS MUCH AS **100 ELEPHANTS.**

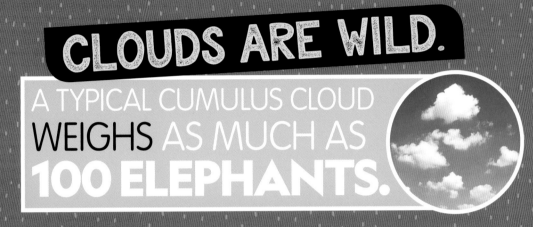

AT ANY GIVEN MOMENT THERE ARE **2,000** **THUNDERSTORMS** OCCURRING ON EARTH.

A PYROCUMULUS CLOUD = A CUMULUS CLOUD FORMED BY THE HOT AIR FROM **WILDFIRES**

155

We all
SCREAM for
ICE CREAM.

SOME **ANCIENT ROMANS** ATE **SNOW SWEETENED** WITH **FRUIT** OR **HONEY.**

AT **7.5 GALLONS** (28 L) PER PERSON A YEAR, **NEW ZEALAND** CONSUMES THE **MOST ICE CREAM** OF ANY COUNTRY.

CHINESE EMPERORS LIVING OVER **1,000 YEARS AGO** MADE WHAT MAY HAVE BEEN THE **FIRST DAIRY ICE CREAM** FROM COW, GOAT, AND BUFFALO MILK.

Literally!

SPIDERS EAT A
TON OF FOOD.

On average, **a spider eats** **2,000** **insects** annually.

Spiders collectively eat as much as **882 million tons** (800 million t) of **prey** every year.

The **weight of insects** annually consumed by spiders is about the same as the **combined weight of all humans** living on Earth.

YOUR **FAVORITE DUOS** DIDN'T ALWAYS GO HAND IN HAND.

THE **POP-UP TOASTER** WAS INVENTED IN **1919**, BUT **PRE-SLICED** BREAD WASN'T SOLD UNTIL **1928**.

PEANUT BUTTER WAS INVENTED IN THE **1880s**, BUT THE JELLY WE USE IN OUR **PB&J** SANDWICHES WASN'T INVENTED UNTIL **1917**.

YOU COULD **WATCH A TV IN 1927** BUT YOU COULDN'T USE **A REMOTE** TO TURN IT ON UNTIL **1950**.

161

THE SPEED

OF LIGHT IS

186,000

miles per second (300,000 km/s). At that speed, you could ...

... circle Earth
7.5 times in one second.

Earth

... get to the galaxy **next door**
in **25,000** years.

Andromeda

... reach the farthest galaxy **(that we know of) in 13.4 billion years.**

GN-Z11

CHEETAHS CAN RUN UP TO

60 MILES AN HOUR

(96.5 KM/H).

That's almost **THREE TIMES** as fast as the **WORLD'S FASTEST HUMAN** ...

... and only **HALF** as fast as a **SKYDIVER.**

A cheetah can **REACH FULL SPEED** in just **THREE SECONDS.**

165

THE ROSETTE-NOSED CHAMELEON CAN SHOOT OUT ITS TONGUE AT A SPEED OF ABOUT **8,500 FEET** PER SECOND (2,600 M PER SECOND).

THAT'S AN ACCELERATION OF UP TO **264 TIMES** THE FORCE OF GRAVITY.

THAT'S **88 TIMES** AS FAST AS THE **ACCELERATION** OF NASA'S SPACE SHUTTLE PROPELLING INTO **ORBIT.**

AMAZING ANIMAL
TONGUES

Like us, animals use their tongues to eat and drink—and occasionally to clown for the camera. But some animals have superweird tongues that go above and beyond the basics.

Chameleons' tongues are not only fast; they're also mind-bogglingly long—up to one and a half times their body length! A sticky mucus 400 times thicker than human saliva sits on the end of these extended appendages, helping the lizards snag and reel in their unsuspecting insect prey.

Sun bears roll out their 10-inch (25-cm)-long tongues to dig out treats from tight spots—especially the yummy bugs that scurry under logs in the forests of southern China where they live. Anteaters can consume up to 30,000 ants and termites every day with their two-foot (0.6-m)-long, spaghetti-shaped tongues, which are covered in a sticky saliva perfect for capturing insects.

Some animals use their tongues to deceive their predators or their prey. The alligator snapping turtle—the largest freshwater turtle in North America—has a piece of red flesh at the end of its tongue that looks like a worm. When curious frogs and fish passing by move in to investigate, the ready reptile snatches them up. Talk about licking the competition!

Anteater

TOTAL SOLAR ECLIPSES AREN'T RARE.

A total solar eclipse happens somewhere on **Earth** about every **18 MONTHS.**

That's about **52 TIMES** in an **average American's life.**

But **in your town,** a total solar eclipse is visible only about once every

400 YEARS.

And in **650 MILLION** years, a total solar eclipse will be very rare; it won't be visible at all because the moon is slowly drifting away from Earth.

More moon, more
HOWLING!

What's the HURRY?

SLOTHS ARE **SLOW.**

172

SLOTHS MOVE **SIX** TO **EIGHT FEET** (1.8 TO 2.4 M) PER MINUTE— **SLOWER THAN SOME SEA STARS.**

THEY **MOVE SO INFREQUENTLY** THAT **ALGAE GROW** ON THEIR FURRY COATS.

THEY EVEN **DIGEST SLOWLY;** THEY LEAVE THE TREE CANOPY ONLY ONCE A WEEK TO **POOP!**

Who you calling SLOWPOKE?

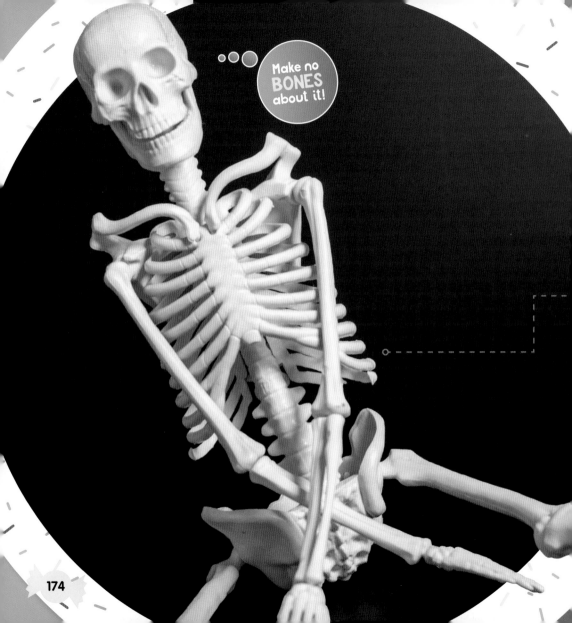

YOUR SKELETON IS EERILY COMPLEX.

Humans are **BORN** with around **300 BONES.** But **ADULTS** have only **206.**

The bones in your **HANDS** and **WRIST** make up **ONE QUARTER** of all the bones in your body.

The **ONLY BONE** in your body not directly **CONNECTED** to another is at the **BASE** of your **TONGUE.**

Every **SEVEN YEARS**, your body has formed a completely **NEW SKELETON.**

SOME ANIMALS HAVE EXTREME ADAPTATIONS.

THE AXOLOTL, a Mexican salamander, can **regenerate pieces** of its brain and heart.

All heart, EXTRA BRAINS!

To scare away approaching predators, **EURASIAN ROLLER NESTLINGS vomit** a smelly orange liquid.

SCORPIONS can go up to a year without eating.

In the winter, **two-thirds of an ALASKAN WOOD FROG freezes solid** and its heart stops beating.

COCKROACHES can **withstand forces 900 TIMES** their body weight **without injury.**

177

STONE AGE HUMANS WERE ARTISTIC.

I'm ready for my CLOSE-UP!

Scientists discovered **40,000-YEAR-OLD FLUTES** made of bird bones and mammoth ivory in a European cave.

The world's **OLDEST HUMAN HAND STENCIL**—also 40,000 years old—was found in a cave in Indonesia.

CAVE PAINTINGS of lions, rhinos, horses, deer, and bison date back to about 30,000 years ago.

ANIMALS CAN BE SUPER **LOUD.**

DOG SQUEAKY TOYS ARE AS LOUD AS LAWN MOWERS.

A BLUE WHALE'S CALL IS LOUDER THAN A JET AT TAKEOFF.

Time for an ENCORE!

BY RUBBING ITS WINGS TOGETHER, A CRICKET PRODUCES A SOUND AS LOUD AS A ROCK CONCERT.

ELEPHANTS MAKE RUMBLING SOUNDS THAT CAN BE HEARD BY OTHER ELEPHANTS UP TO SIX MILES (10 KM) AWAY.

THE SAHARA IS EXTREME.

Parts of the Sahara **receive less than one inch** (2.5 cm) of rain each year.

Nighttime temperatures in the Sahara are about the same as **summer temperatures** in the **Arctic.**

Even the **animals are extreme:** SuperCroc, a **crocodile-like** animal **as long as a bus,** roamed what is now the Sahara **110 million** years ago.

All
ABOARD!

CAMELS:
TAKING THE HEAT

There's a reason camels earned the nickname "ships of the desert." For nearly 2,000 years, they have helped people move goods and supplies through the Saharan landscape, which can reach temperatures above 130°F (54°C). How do they do it? Camels can guzzle 30 gallons (114 L) of water at a time, then walk for 17 days without drinking another drop—or eating. That's a major advantage when traversing a land that receives as little as one inch (2.5 cm) of rain a year in some parts.

Camels have unique adaptations that are key to their success in withstanding the desert conditions and managing hard work. That hump on an Arabian camel's back isn't a holding tank for water; it stores up to 80 pounds (36 kg) of fat! When food is scarce, the fat breaks down into water and energy to keep the camel going. If a camel's hump droops, it means fat levels are low—but the hump will stand up again once the camel has eaten and rested. Other excellent desert adaptations: nostrils that close to keep the sand out, two rows of long eyelashes to protect their eyes from blowing sand, and supertough lips that can withstand thorny desert vegetation. And their thick toe pads were made for walking, allowing them to cruise through rocky terrain and sand at speeds of 10 miles an hour (16 km/h) for a steady 18 hours. Talk about all-terrain transportation!

LUNCH-
time
already?

186

TIME PASSES FASTER THE HIGHER UP YOU ARE.

A year on **MOUNT EVEREST** lasts **15 MICROSECONDS** longer than one at **SEA LEVEL.**

But even though they're **HIGH UP**, astronauts in space actually **AGE MORE SLOWLY** than people on Earth because they're moving **SO QUICKLY.**

An astronaut who spends **10 YEARS** on the International Space Station will be **0.1 SECOND YOUNGER** when she returns.

I'm young at HEART!

187

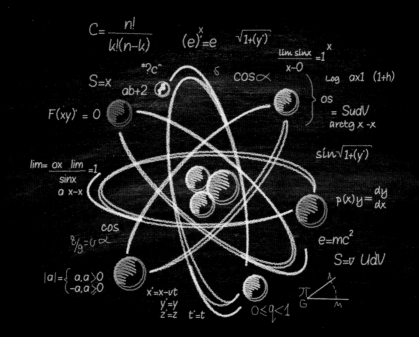

ATOMS ARE

TINY.

AN ATOM IS **ONE TEN-MILLIONTH OF A MILLIMETER** WIDE.

A **SINGLE HUMAN HAIR** IS APPROXIMATELY AS WIDE AS **500,000 ATOMS** STACKED ON TOP OF ONE ANOTHER.

SMALL
but
powerful!

99.9999999999996%
OF AN ATOM IS
EMPTY SPACE.

THE CENTER OF THE EARTH IS A LONG WAY DOWN.

You'd have to dig a hole
3,959 MILES (6,371 km) **DEEP** to reach the center of the Earth.

If you could **jump in a tunnel** that went to the **center of the planet,** you would be

FREE-FALLING FOR 19 MINUTES.

The center of the Earth is so far down that the **pressure at its inner core** is more than

THREE MILLION TIMES

the **pressure at Earth's surface.**

WATER IS EVERYWHERE!

Almost **three-quarters** of **Earth's surface** is covered in water.

The **human brain** is **75 percent** water.

A **thunderhead cloud** can hold more than **2 billion pounds** (907,184,740 kg) of **water**.

NATURAL DISASTERS ARE
FURIOUS FORCES.

Erupting volcanoes can **throw rocks** at speeds up to **800 miles** an hour (1,287 km/h).

A **Category 5 hurricane** generates winds that can travel more than **200 miles** an hour (322 km/h).

A **tsunami** can move across the ocean at the same speed as a **Boeing 747.**

A **tropical cyclone** can release as much energy as **10,000 nuclear bombs.**

A magnitude **9 earthquake** releases about as much energy as **99,000,000 tons** (89,811,289 t) of TNT does.

It's all
RELATIVE!

HUMANS ARE CLOSELY RELATED TO THE
GREAT APES.

The **GENETIC DIFFERENCE** between **HUMANS** and **CHIMPANZEES** is **ABOUT** **1%.**

That's only **10 TIMES** the genetic difference between **INDIVIDUAL HUMANS.**

And some **SCIENTISTS** believe that **HUMANS** and **BONOBOS** may be even **MORE CLOSELY RELATED.**

NEW YORK'S CENTRAL PARK
IS CHOCK-FULL OF

HISTORY.

IN THE EARLY **1800s,** THE AREA WHERE CENTRAL PARK NOW STANDS WAS A SETTLEMENT CALLED **SENECA VILLAGE.**

IT WAS **DESIGNED** WITH CURVED ROADS TO **DISCOURAGE**

HORSE AND CARRIAGE RACING.

THE PARK'S **OLDEST MONUMENT** IS A 3,500-YEAR-OLD ANCIENT EGYPTIAN OBELISK CALLED **CLEOPATRA'S NEEDLE.**

I'm just **HORSING** around!

INDEX

Boldface indicates illustrations.

A

Adaptations, animal 176–177, 185
Africa
  true size 26, **26**, 27, **27**, 29
  tsetse flies 57, **57**
  see also Sahara
African gray parrots 105, **105**
Ageusia 11
Aging: in space 187
Airplanes 35, **35**, 86–87, **86–87**
Alaska, U.S.A. 49, 98–99, **98–99**, 101
Alcatraz Island, California, U.S.A. **38**, 39
Algae 173
Alligator snapping turtles 169
Almonds 47, **47**
Alpha Centauri A and B (stars) 111
Andromeda (galaxy) 163, **163**
Anglerfish **72**
Antarctica 29, 146–147, **146–147**
Anteaters 169, **169**
Ants 7, **7**, **120**, 121, **121**, 169
Appendixes 123
Arctic regions 144–145, **144–145**
Art: cave paintings **178–179**, 179

Astronauts
  aging 187
  food in space 107, 109
  G-forces 16, 55
  moon missions 129
  sleeping bags **108**, 109
Atoms **188**, 188–189
Australia
  beaches 62–63, **62–63**
  deadly species **66–67**, 67
  desert 63, **63**
  lost dog 15
  unusual animals 64–65, **64–65**
Avocados 47, 125, **125**
Axolotls 176, **176**

B

Babies 25, **25**
Baby animals
  elephants 117, **117**
  koalas 117, **117**
Bags, plastic 151
Bananas 47, **47, 77**
Banjos 39, **39**
Baseballs 68–69, **68–69**
Bats **90**, 91
Beaches 62–63, **62–63,** 129
Beetles 45, **45**
Berries 46–47, **47**
Billion (number) 8–9
Bioluminescent animals 72, 73, **73**
Bird bones 179

Birds
  African gray parrots 105, **105**
  chickens 105, **105**
  common swifts 105, **105**
  Eurasian rollers 177, **177**
  flamingos **104–105**, 105
  frigatebirds 105, **105**
  hummingbirds 81, **81**
  kingfishers **44**, 45
Birthdays 12–13
Bison **125**, 179
Black light 73
Blackberries 46
Blinking 81
Blue-ringed octopuses 57, **57**
Blue whales 24–25, **24–25,** 181
Bones
  bird 179
  human **174–175**, 175
Bonobos 197, **197**
Books **81**, 133, 153, **153**
Brain, human 123, 193, **193**
Bread
  banned on International Space Station 107, 109
  pre-sliced 160
  rye 77, **77**
  toast **76, 160**
Breathing 119
Bullet trains 45, **45**
Burj Khalifa, Dubai, U.A.E. 127, **127**

C

Camels **184,** 185, **185**
Capone, Al 39
Car racing 16–17, **16–17**
Cashews 47
Cats 15, **15, 52,** 53, **53,** 78, **78**
Cave paintings **178–179,** 179
Central Park, New York City
    198–199, 199
Challenger Deep, Pacific
    Ocean 35
Chameleons 166, **166–167,** 169
Cheetahs **164–165,** 165
Chickens 105, **105**
Chimpanzees **196,** 197
Chinese emperors 157
Cilantro 11, **11**
Cleaning hacks 77
Cleopatra's Needle
    (monument), New York
    City 199, **199**
Clouds **154,** 155, **155,** 193, **193**
Cockroaches 177, **177**
Cold, common 135
Cold viruses 134
Comics **70,** 71
Common swifts 105, **105**
Computers 88–89, **89**
Cone snails **56,** 57
Coral 73, **73**
Corned-beef sandwiches 107,
    107
Crickets 181, **181**
Criminals 39
Cumulus clouds 155, **155**
Cyclones 195, **195**
Cycloseris erosa 73, **73**

D

Deer 179
Delaware, U.S.A. 101
Delaware River, U.S.A. 69
Deserts **26–27,** 45, 63, **63,**
    182–184, 185
Dew 45
Dictionaries 131, **131**
Divers **34,** 83
Dog squeaky toys 181
Dogs 15, **15, 50,** 50–51, **51,** 78
Donkeys 83, **83**
Draco lizards 141, **141**
Duck-billed platypuses 65,
    65, 67, **67**
Dutch people 122

E

Earth (planet)
    closest stars 111
    core 37, **37,** 190–191, **190–191**
    population 48–49
    solar eclipses 170–171,
        170–171
    surface 191, 193
Earthquakes 195, **195**
Earwax spoons 83, **83**
Echolocation 91
Eclipses 170–171, **170–171**
Eggs
    octopuses 117
    platypuses 65, 67
    termites 97
Eggshells 83, **83**
Egyptians, ancient 83
Elephants 78, **78,** 117, **117,** 181,
    181
Elizabeth II, Queen (United
    Kingdom) 61
Empire State Building, New
    York City 127, **127**
Eurasian rollers 177, **177**
Everest, Mount, China-Nepal
    35, **35,** 93, **93, 186,** 187
Evolution 122–123
Eyebrows 30
Eyelashes 30

F

Fingernails 57, 115
Fireflies 45, **45,** 73, **73**
Fireworks 136, **136–137**
Fish
    anglerfish **72**
    in Arctic regions 144
    goldfish 9, **9**
    mandarin fish 73, **73**
    as symbols 115
Flamingos **104–105,** 105
Flu viruses 134
Flutes 179
Flying snakes 141, **141**
Food
    hot dogs 142–143, **142–143**
    hot sauce 107, **107**
    ice cream **60,** 61, **156,**
        156–157, **157**

INDEX

noodles 32–33, **32–33**
pizza **22–23,** 23, 153, **153**
potatoes **148,** 149, **149**
seeds 47, **47**
in space 107, 109
yogurt 77, **77**
see also Bread; Fruits;
Sandwiches
Fourth of July celebrations
136
Francis, Pope 61
Frigatebirds 105, **105**
Frogs
turtle frogs 65, **65**
wood frogs 177, **177**
Fruits 46–47, **46–47**; *see also*
Bananas; Grapes; Tomatoes

G
G-forces 16, 55
Gadsby (Wright) 133
Galaxies 163, **163**
Genetics 11, 197
Germs 31; *see also* Viruses
Globes 29
GN-z11 (galaxy) **163**
Goats 18, **18,** 157
Goldfish 9, **9**
Googol (number) 21
Googolplex (number) 21
Grapes 115, **115**
Great apes **196,** 197, **197**
Greece, ancient 7
Green peas 47, **47**

Greenland 27, **27**
Ground sloths **124,** 125

H
Hair
human 30–31, **30–31,** 189,
189
pig 83
Hamsters **14,** 15, **15**
Hand stencil, world's oldest
179
"Happy Birthday" (song) 13
Hares **58–59,** 59
Haunted places 39
Hawaiian Islands, North
Pacific Ocean 95
Heart, human 119, **119**
Henry VII, King (England)
136, **136**
Honeydews 121, **121**
Horse and carriage racing 199
Horses 179, **199**
Hot dogs 142–143, **142–143**
Hot sauce 107, **107**
Human ancestors 9
Human body
brain 123, 193, **193**
breathing 119
evolution 122–123
hair 30–31, **30–31,** 189, **189**
heart 119, **119**
skeleton **174–175,** 175
skin cells 119
spit 119

taste buds 10, 11
teeth 82–83, 123, 153
Hummingbirds 81, **81**
Humpback whales 46, **46**
Hurricanes 195, **195**
Hyams Beach, Australia 63, **63**
Hybrid plants 149, **149**
Hyenas 78, **78**

I
Ice cream **60,** 61, **156,** 156–157,
157
Icebergs 147
Indonesia: Stone Age art 179
Inland taipans **66,** 67
Insects 96–97, **96–97,** 159
ants 7, **7, 120,** 121, **121,** 169
beetles 45, **45**
crickets 181, **181**
fireflies 45, **45,** 73, **73**
locusts 97
termites 97, 169
tsetse flies 57, **57**
Instant noodles 32, **32,** 33
International Space Station
106, 107, 109, 187
Inventors and inventions
airplane 87
bullet trains 45
hot dogs 143
jelly 161
LED lights 45
peanut butter 161
pop-up toasters 160

TV remotes 161
water collecting systems
45
wind turbines 45

J

Japan
    bullet trains 45, **45**
    noodle-cup theater 33
Jelly 109, **160–161,** 161
Jobs: world leaders 61
Jupiter (planet) 42, **43**

K

Kangaroos 64, **64**
Kingfishers **44,** 45
Kish, Daniel 91, **91**
Koalas 117, **117**

L

LED lights 45, **45**
Lemons 121, **121**
Light, speed of 162
Lightbulbs 45, **45**
Lightning 37, **155**
Lions 179, **179**
Lipograms 133
Lizards
    chameleons 166, **166–167,**
    169
    Draco lizards 141, **141**
Locusts 97
Luck 115, 139

M

Madagascar 61
Mammoth ivory 179
Manatees 78, **79**
Mandarin fish 73, **73**
Mapmaking 29
Mars (planet): volcano 95, **95**
Mauna Loa (volcano), Hawaii,
    U.S.A. 92–93, **92–93**
Megarodent 125
Megatherium americanum
    124, 125
Mercator projection 29
Mice, computer 89
Microgravity 107, 109
Middle Ages 83
Milk 157
Million (number) 6–7
Millipedes 73, **73**
Moon 35, **128,** 129, **170,** 171
Mud 69

N

Narwhals **102,** 103
NASCAR 16–17, **16–17**
Natural disasters 194–195,
    194–195
New Year's Eve 115
New Zealand 49, **49**
Niagara Falls, Canada-U.S.
    80, 81
Night sky 111
Night vision 53
Nightshade family 149
Noodles 32–33, **32–33**

North Pole 29
Nose hairs 31
Numbers 6–9, 20–21
Nuts 47, **47**

O

Obama, Barack **60,** 61
Obelisks 199, **199**
Ocean
    currents 75
    deepest point 35
    tsunamis 195, **195**
    underwater volcanoes
    92, 93
Octopuses 57, **57, 116,** 117
Olympics 7
Olympus Mons (volcano),
    Mars 95, **95**
Ox hooves 83

P

Peanut butter and jelly
    sandwiches 109, **160–161,**
    161
Photography 40–41
Picky eaters 11
Pig hair 83
Pizza **22–23,** 23, 153, **153**
Plastic garbage 151
Poop
    koalas 117
    sloths 173
Potatoes **148,** 149, **149**
Prehistoric animals 124–125,
    124–125

INDEX

extinct rhino 103, **103**
pterosaurs **140,** 141
SuperCroc 183, **183**
T. rex 105, **105**
Prisons and prisoners **38,** 39
Pterosaurs **140,** 141
Pyrocumulus clouds 155, **155**

R
Racing
    horse and carriage 199
    stock car 16–17, **16–17**
Rainforests 125, 146
Reading 81, 153
Remote controls 161
Reptiles, flying **140,** 140–141, **141**
Rhinoceroses
    cave paintings 179
    extinct species 103, **103**
Rhode Island, U.S.A. 100–101, **100–101**
Robocup 139, **139**
Rodent, world's largest 125
Roller coasters 54–55, **55**
Romans, ancient 157
Rosette-nosed chameleons 166, **166–167**
Rubber ducks 74–75, **74–75**
Rubik's Cube 81, **81**
Rye bread 77, **77**

S
Saber-toothed cats 125
Sahara, Africa **26–27,** 27, 182–183, **182–183,** 185
Salamanders 176, **176**
Sandwiches
    corned-beef 107, **107**
    peanut butter and jelly 109, **160–161**
Scorpions 177, **177**
Scotland 103
Sea stars 173, **173**
Seeds 47, **47,** 144
Selfies 41
Sheep 19, **19**
Shipwrecks 83
Shoes 112–113, **112–113**
"Siberian unicorns" 103, **103**
Silver 77
Skeleton, human **174–175,** 175
Skin cells 119
Skydivers 165, **165**
Skyscrapers 126–127, **126–127**
Sleeping bags **108,** 109
Sleeping sickness 58
Sloths **124,** 125, **172,** 173, **173**
Smell, sense of 51
Snakes
    flying 141, **141**
    largest ever 125, **125**
    most venomous 67
Snow 157
Soap 11, **11**
Soccer 138–139, **138–139**

Solar eclipses 170–171, **170–171**
Solar system 94, 129
Sound
    echolocation 91
    speed of 84–85
Sounds, animal 91, 181
South Africa: roller coaster 55
South America
    on maps 29
    prehistoric animals **124,** 125
Space
    eating food in 106–107, 109
    International Space Station hacks 109
    slower aging in 187
Space Needle, Seattle, Washington, U.S.A. 126, **126**
Space shuttles 16, 55, 166, **166**
Spain: superstitions 115
Spiders 57, **57,** 67, 158–159, **158–159**
Spit 119
Squeaky toys 181
Stars 111
Stone Age 9, 179
Strawberries 46, **46–47**
Sun **36–37,** 37, **110,** 111; *see also* Solar eclipses
Sun bears **168,** 169
Sunburn 77
SuperCroc 183, **183**
Superman (character) **70,** 71
Supernovae 37, **37**
Superstitions 115

Supertasters 11
Sweat 30, 53, 107
Sydney funnel-web spiders 57, **57**

T
T. rex 105, **105**
Tails
    goats 18, **18**
    platypuses **65,** 67
    sheep 19, **19**
Taste, sense of 11, 107
Taste buds 10–11, 51
Teeth 82–83, 123, 153
Televisions 161, **161**
Termites 97, 169
Thailand: floating soccer field **138–139,** 139
Thunderhead clouds 193, **193**
Thunderstorms 155, **155**
Time 42, 187
Titanoboa 125, **125**
Toasters 160, **160**
Toenails 115
Tomatoes 47, **148,** 149, **149**
Tongue clicks 91
Tongues, animal
    anteaters 169, **169**
    chameleons 166, **166–167,** 169
    sun bears **168,** 169
Tongues, human **10,** 175, **175**
Toothaches 83
Toothbrushes **82,** 83, **153**
Toothpaste 83
Toothpicks 83, **83**

Tortoises 59, **59**
Toys, squeaky 181
Trash 150–151, **150–151**
Tropical cyclones 195, **195**
Tsetse flies 57, **57**
Tsunamis 195, **195**
Turtle frogs 65, **65**
Turtles 169

U
Underwear 139
Unicorns 103, **103**
United States
    Fourth of July celebrations 136
    haunted places 39
    hot dog consumption 142
    most common birthdays 13
    potato consumption 149
    waste production 151
    see also Alaska; Delaware; Rhode Island
Urine 107

V
Vampire squid 73, **73**
Vegetables, most popular 149
Venom 57, 67
Vestigial body parts 123
Viruses 134, 135
Vision loss 91
Volcanoes 194, **194–195**; *see also* Mauna Loa; Olympus Mons

W
Water
    astronauts 107
    camels 185
    collecting systems 45
    dogs' taste buds 51
    Earth's surface 193
    human brain 193
    speed of sound through 85
    thunderhead clouds 193
Waterfalls **80,** 81
Whales
    blue whales 24–25, **24–25,** 181
    humpback whales 46, **46**
Wichita Falls, Texas, U.S.A. 126, **126**
Wildfires 155, **155**
Wind turbines 46, **46**
Wisdom teeth 123
Wood
    first computer mouse 89
    knocking on 115
    speed of sound through 85
Wood frogs 177, **177**
Words 81, 130–131, 133
Wright, Ernest Vincent **132,** 133
Writing 133

Y
Yawning 153, **153**
Yogurt 77, **77**

PHOTO CREDITS

Cover (UP RT), SSSCCC/SS; (candy letters), Henk Dawson; (LO RT), Erik Lam/SS; (LO LE), Kevkhiev Yury/DT; (pizza), bestv/SS; (ball), irin-k/SS; (UP LE), DM7/SS; spine, Erik Lam/SS; back cover (mouse), Rudmer Zwerver/SS; (lollipop), Volodymyr Krasyuk/SS; (LE), Ruth Black/SS; (CTR), Andrey Pavlov/DT; (RT), Photo by DEA/V. Pirozzi/De Agostini/GI

Interior 1 (mouse), Rudmer Zwerver/SS; 1 (lollipop), Volodymyr Krasyuk/SS; 1 (LO), Sergey_Peterman/GI; 2, tea maeklong/SS; 3 (candy letters), Henk Dawson; 4, Erik Lam/SS; 5 (CTR LE), Elenamiv/SS; 5 (LO LE), irin-k/SS; 5 (LO CTR), Ziva_K/GI; 5 (LO RT), robert_s/SS; 6 (Background), LUMIKK555/SS; 7 (LE), Photo by DEA/V. Pirozzi/De Agostini/GI; 7 (UP RT), Andrey Pavlov/DT; 7 (LO RT), Ruth Black/SS; 8 (Background), EFKS/SS; 8 (LO), Javier Brosch/SS; 9 (UP RT), Aaron Amat/SS; 9 (CTR LE), Irochka_T/GI; 9 (LO), bloodua/GI; 10, wundervisuals/GI; 11 (UP RT), matkub2499/SS; 11 (CTR RT), oksana2010/SS; 11 (LO LE), Sinisa Botas/SS; 12 (UP), barbaliss/SS; 12 (LO), tobkatrina/SS; 13 (UP RT), Ermolaev Alexander/SS; 13 (LO), Flynt/DT; 13 (CTR LE), Ljupco Smokovski/SS; 14, otsphoto/SS; 15 (UP LE), Javier Brosch/SS; 15 (sticker), ducu59us/SS; 15 (CTR RT), SJ Allen/SS; 15 (LO), anyamuse/SS; 16-17, action sports/SS; 18, Eric Isselee/SS; 19, Innaastakhova/DT; 20, Plateresca/SS; 21 (CTR), Susan Schmitz/SS; 21 (LO CTR), Srijaroen/SS; 21 (LO LE), Garsya/SS; 22, IsuaneyeSS; 23, Mookyoung Jeong/SS; 24, David Fleetham/Nature Picture Library; 25 (UP LE), wong sze yuen/SS; 25 (CTR RT), Inara Prusakova/SS; 25 (LO), ASDF_MEDIA/SS; 26, Gallo Images - Heinrich van den Berg/GI; 26, NG Maps; 27, Anton Petrus/SS; 27 (RT), NG Maps; 28, NG Maps; 29 (mouse), Rudmer Zwerver/SS; 29 (lollipop), Volodymyr Krasyuk/SS; 31, Evan Kafka/GI; 31 (UP RT), Eric Isselee/SS; 32, Somrerk Witthayanant/SS; 33 (UP LE), EDU Vision/ASP; 33 (CTR RT), Melica/SS; 33 (LO RT), Jagodka/SS; 34, Images & Stories/ASP; 34 (LO), Lobroart/SS; 35 (UP RT), Yongyut Kumsri/SS; 35 (CTR LE), SVStudio/SS; 35 (LO RT), vitec/SS; 36-37, PRIMA/SS; 36 (CTR LE), Ermolaev Alexander/SS; 37 (CTR RT), Andrea Danti/SS; 37 (LO LE), NASA, ESA, G. Bacon (STScI); 38, f11photo/SS; 39 (CTR LE), koya979/SS; 39 (CTR RT), Ingram; 39 (LO), rangizzz/SS; 40, guteksk7/SS; 41, FotoYakov/SS; 42 (UP RT), Sashkin/SS; 42 (LO LE), billdayone/SS; 43, David Aguilar; 43 (LO RT), Visual Generation/SS; 44, PongMoji/SS; 45 (UP RT), Yann hubert/SS; 45 (LO RT), Okawa Photo/SS; 45 (beetle), Solvin Zankl/Nature Picture Library; 45 (CTR), Kamonrat/SS; 45 (CTR LE), Chones/SS; 45 (UP CTR), Brandon Alms/SS; 46, Ewa Studio/SS; 47 (UP RT), Dionisvera/SS; 47 (LO RT), mayakovaSS; 47 (LO LE), Aleksey Troshin/SS; 47 (UP LE), Maks Narodenko/SS; 48, PaulPaladin/SS; 49 (trees), Kittichai/SS; 49 (people), Rawpixel.com/SS; 49 (CTR LE), Anton Balazh/SS; 49 (LO RT), robert_s/SS; 50, TheDogPhotographer/GI; 51 (LE), Celig/SS; 51 (UP RT), Andrey_Kuzmin/SS; 51 (LO), WilleeCole Photography/SS; 52, kapulya/GI; 53 (LE), by CaoWei/GI; 53 (RT), Greenery/SS; 55, KJimages/GI; 56, Cyhel/SS; 57 (UP RT), imageBROKER/SS; 57 (CTR LE), The Natural History Museum/ASP; 57 (LO RT), Yusran Abdul Rahman/SS; 58, Daria Medvedeva/SS; 59 (LE), Eric Isselee/SS; 59 (RT), Tracy Hebden/DT; 60, EDB Image Archive/ASP; 61 (UP LE), Photodisc; 61 (UP RT), Bryan Solomon/SS; 61 (LO), unpict/SS; 62, Johan Larson/SS; 63 (UP), Edward Haylan/SS; 63 (LO), Paul Nevin/GI; 64, Jan Pokorn/DT; 65 (UP), Dave Watts/ASP; 65 (LO), ANT Photo Library/Science Source; 66, Susan Schmitz/SS; 67 (LE), Roland Seitre/Minden Pictures; 67 (RT), Fairfax Media/Fairfax Media via GI; 68-69, Hidehiro Kigawa/GI; 70, Heritage Auctions, Dallas; 71 (LE), Brand X; 71 (RT), Peter Spirer/DT; 72, superjoseph/SS; 73 (UP), Steve Downer/Science Source; 73 (CTR RT), khlungcenter/SS; 73 (LO RT), Danté Fenolio/Science Source; 73 (LO LE), Howard Chew/ASP; 73 (CTR LE), Ted Kinsman/Science Source; 74-75, Press Association via AP Images; 76, harmpeti/SS; 77 (UP RT), MaraZe/SS; 77 (CTR RT), classpics/GI; 77 (LO LE), Maks Narodenko/SS; 77 (CTR LE), yuda chen/SS; 78 (UP RT), Anan Kaewkhammul/SS; 78 (CTR LE), Elena Rudyk/SS; 78 (LO LE), Talvi/SS; 79, Greg Amptman/SS; 80, TRphotos/SS; 81 (UP LE), StevenRussellSmithPhotos/SS; 81 (CTR RT), PeterVrabel/SS; 81 (LO LE), Mik122/GI; 82, oksana2010/SS; 83 (UP RT), Carol Tedesco/Florida Keys News Bureau via GI/GI; 83 (LO CTR), Red2000 Creative/SS; 83 (LO LE), alfernec/SS; 84-85, Henrik Sorensen/GI; 86 (UP), Carlos Yudica/SS; 86 (LO), filo/GI; 87, Library of Congress Prints and Photographs Division; 88, jamesteohart/SS; 89 (mouse), Rudmer Zwerver/SS;

CREDITS

Since 1888, the National Geographic Society has funded more than 12,000 research, exploration, and preservation projects around the world. The Society receives funds from National Geographic Partners, LLC, funded in part by your purchase. A portion of the proceeds from this book supports this vital work. To learn more, visit natgeo.com/info.

NATIONAL GEOGRAPHIC and Yellow Border Design are trademarks of the National Geographic Society, used under license.

For more information, visit nationalgeographic.com, call 1-800-647-5463, or write to the following address:

National Geographic Partners
1145 17th Street N.W.
Washington, D.C. 20036-4688 U.S.A.

Visit us online at nationalgeographic.com/books

For librarians and teachers: ngchildrensbooks.org

More for kids from National Geographic: natgeokids.com

National Geographic Kids magazine inspires children to explore their world with fun yet educational articles on animals, science, nature, and more. Using fresh storytelling and amazing photography, *Nat Geo Kids* shows kids ages 6 to 14 the fascinating truth about the world—and why they should care. kids.nationalgeographic.com/subscribe

For information about special discounts for bulk purchases, please contact National Geographic Books Special Sales: specialsales@natgeo.com

For rights or permissions inquiries, please contact National Geographic Books Subsidiary Rights: bookrights@natgeo.com

Designed by Amanda Larsen and Julide Dengel

Trade paperback ISBN: 978-1-4263-3437-5
Reinforced library binding ISBN: 978-1-4263- 3438-2

The publisher would like to thank Julie Beer, author; Chelsea Lin, author; Jen Agresta, project manager; Rebecca Baines, editorial director; Paige Towler, project editor; Michelle Tyler, project editor; Sarah J. Mock, senior photo editor; Joan Gossett, production editor; and Anne LeongSon and Gus Tello, design production assistants.

Printed in China
19/PPS/1

How SWEET!